Robert D

REFORMED

What It Means • Why It Matters

FAITH
ALIVE®
Christian Resources

Grand Rapids, Michigan

Faith Alive Christian Resources published by CRC
Publications.
Reformed: What It Means, Why It Matters, © 2001
by CRC Publications, 2850 Kalamazoo Ave. SE,
Grand Rapids, MI 49560. All rights reserved. With
the exception of brief excerpts for review purposes,
no part of this book may be reproduced in any
manner whatsoever without written permission
from the publisher. Printed in the United States of
America on recycled paper. ✪

We welcome your comments. Call us at
1-800-333-8300 or e-mail us at
editors@faithaliveresources.org.

Library of Congress Cataloging-in-Publication Data
DeMoor, Robert, 1950-
    Reformed: what it means, why it matters/
  Robert DeMoor.
      p.   cm.
    ISBN 1-56212-433-1
    1. Reformed Church. I. Title
  BX9422.3 D4 2001
  285–dc21   2001045010

10 9 8 7 6 5 4 3 2 1

Contents

Welcome!

We're glad you're joining us on our brief arm-chair tour of what it means to be Reformed. Who are Reformed Christians? What do they believe? How are they different from other Christians?

You may have any number of reasons for asking these questions:

- *Maybe you're a new Christian looking for a church to join.* You want to be sure you know what you're getting into, so you're taking a careful look at what Reformed denominations teach and practice. Good for you! It's important for you to know what a church stands for so that you can make an informed choice. For more information and answers to your specific questions, talk to the pastor, small group leader, or person who invited you to this church. They'll be eager to talk with you about Reformed teaching and to refer you to someone else if they don't have the answers you're looking for.

- *Maybe you're considering studying or teaching at a school or college that promotes itself as being "Reformed."* You want to know more about the contours of the Reformed Christian faith

FACTOID

A lot of Reformed denominations put the word "Reformed" right in their name. Most of those churches came from continental Europe. Others call themselves "Presbyterian." Presbyterian churches are Reformed churches that hail from Scotland. While Reformed and Presbyterian churches have adopted some different statements of faith, they all subscribe to the same basic church creeds and hold more or less to the same teachings and practices. This book will apply equally well to those who call themselves "Reformed," "Presbyterian," or both.

before you decide. You'll probably want to do more digging, but this booklet may be a good place to start. May God's will in your decision become clear to you!

- *Maybe you're a young person who wants to get serious about making public profession of your faith.* You realize that your commitment is first and foremost to your Lord and Savior. But that commitment unites you to your fellow believers as well. What's unique about the teachings and practices of *this* church? Why do you want to make public profession of faith here in the presence of *these* people? We want to help you answer these important questions.

- *Or maybe you've been a member of a Reformed/Presbyterian church all your life, but you've never thought through why you travel past ten other churches to attend this one.* Maybe a friend or neighbor asked you to explain what being Reformed really means and you couldn't give a clear answer. We hope this pamphlet will help—whether you study it alone or in a small group setting.

So what will this pamphlet talk about? We'll take a look at the main features of the Reformed version of the Christian faith. We'll do that under three headings:

- *Reformed roots:* where we came from (chapter 1).

- *Reformed teachings:* our distinctive beliefs (chapters 2-3).

- *Reformed practice:* the way we do things (chapter 4).

Please keep two things in mind as you survey the distinctive features of the Reformed faith.

First, Reformed Christianity is not some kind of sect or cult. Reformed Christians confess that we are only a small part of a much larger body of believers who love and serve Jesus Christ. We're part of a family that includes Orthodox, Roman Catholic, Anglican, Evangelical, and a host of other churches that confess and practice the Christian faith. This book does not intend to argue that Reformed Christians are better than others. It only tries to point out our distinguishing features—making it easier for you to tell one sibling in God's family from another and helping you find your own place in the body of Christ.

Second, Reformed teachings are shared by other denominations as well. What's different is the emphasis that we might place on them. Cornelius Plantinga writes:

> Our accents lie more on the sovereignty of God, on the authority of Scripture, on the need for disciplined holiness in personal Christian life, and finally, on Christianity as a religion of the Kingdom.

—*A Sure Thing: What We Believe and Why* (Grand Rapids: CRC Publications, 2001), p. 281

WORD ALERT

Sect or *cult* refers to a group of people with two distinguishing traits. One, they hold unique beliefs that are very different from the mainstream. Two, they believe that holding this set of beliefs makes them the only true believers to the exclusion of everyone else.

FAST FORWARD

Maybe you can't take the time to read this whole booklet just now. You know the lingo and you want the Reformed distinctives *now* in a nutshell. Try this one: Some Christians rely heavily on the teachings of people, on human traditions, or on what church assemblies say. The key Reformed notion is that it's WISER to stick to what God teaches in the Bible.

- **W**ord-led—God gives us the Bible as our complete and unfailing guide for faith and life.

- **I**ncluded—although we do nothing to deserve it, God graciously includes us in his family by giving us saving faith that ties us into all that Jesus did and does for us.

- **S**ealed—through the two (and only two) sacraments of baptism and Lord's Supper, God makes our faith grow by visibly confirming what God promises us in the Bible.

- **E**mpowered—through the gift of the Holy Spirit we live a life of daily conversion in which we keep on learning to say no to our own selfish, spoiled-rotten will, and yes to God's good and perfect will.

- **R**eleased—since we don't have to waste our time trying to *earn* our salvation (we can't anyway), God frees us up and gives us the Holy Spirit so we can gratefully spend our lives living the gospel, sharing it with others, and serving God, our neighbors, and our world.

For example, the Reformed faith teaches the Lordship of Jesus Christ over all creation. We can't imagine a Christian church that doesn't hold to that teaching. But Reformed believers place a lot more emphasis on this teaching than many other Christians do. As a result, Reformed believers have invested a lot of their energy and resources in Christian education (Christian day schools, colleges, and seminaries), Christ-centered political/social action, and parachurch ministries to those in need.

As you study this booklet, keep in mind that all Bible-believing Christians share one single language of faith. But, as Plantinga points out, we all speak it with our own accent. Be proud of *your* accent. Thank God for it. Add yours to the rich diversity of tongues that speak of the great things God has done. And offer your unique expression of your faith back to the One who deserves all glory, worship, and praise. "Through Jesus . . . let us continually offer to God a sacrifice of praise—the fruit of lips that confess his name" (Hebrews 13:15).

CHAPTER I

Back to the Beginning

Why the Church Needed Reforming

Two thousand years ago, on Pentecost, God poured out the Holy Spirit. By the power of the Spirit, Jesus' followers began to spread the good news about him worldwide. Where their preaching was heard, churches sprang up. These churches lived the gospel and, in turn, spread it to others as well. As these churches matured, they joined together into an organizational structure that helped them support each other, held them accountable, and kept them on the right track in their teaching. For a thousand years churches were more or less organized under one overarching structure.

During that time the organizational structure of the church hardened and its leaders became corrupt. By the dawn of the second millennium power struggles and doctrinal differences between church leaders split the church into two parts: the Eastern Orthodox Church, headed by the patriarch of the Church of Constantinople, and the Latin Western Church, led by the pope, the bishop of Rome. This church came to be known as the Roman Catholic Church.

FAST FORWARD

Not in the mood to review the "family history"? Skip to the next chapter, "God's in Charge." If you do, keep in mind that these teachings were emphasized so heavily because of the historical context. The Reformers, people like John Calvin and John Knox, needed to correct the abuses of the Roman Catholic Church of their day. When the Roman church refused to change, the Reformers *re-formed* their churches to follow biblical teaching and practices more closely.

By the time the sixteenth century rolled around, many Reformers had tried to correct the teachings and practices of the Roman Catholic Church, calling it back to obedience to God's Word. But the powerful church leadership had managed to suppress these attempts, often by torturing and killing the Reformers.

So what needed reforming? Here's just a partial list:

- Corruption was widespread among the clergy, especially at the top.

- The church tortured people suspected of holding non-orthodox beliefs until they confessed or died.

- The church encouraged believers to pray to Mary and the saints.

- Salesmen for the church went around selling "indulgences"—letters written by the pope supposedly forgiving people their sins. One of these, Tetzel, was heard to proclaim loudly, "The minute your money drops in the box, the soul of your relative jumps out of purgatory into heaven."

During the sixteenth century, though, reform could no longer be stemmed. Many people began to follow and support the Reformers. The Roman Catholic Church could no longer silence or turf out these "Protestants." A number of events came together to place the Bible into the hands of the people in the pew. By having personal access to the Bible, they were able to judge for themselves whether what the church leaders

SO WHAT

Corrupt leadership can severely damage our spiritual growth or keep us from true faith altogether. So *always* pray for your spiritual leaders, encouraging and cooperating with them where you can—but also keep an eye on them to make sure they stay on track, obediently following God's Word and God's will.

were teaching them was actually true. As a result, many believers followed the Reformers out of the Roman Catholic Church in order to return to the teachings of Scripture.

A number of strands of Protestant churches began as a result of the Reformation: Lutheran and Anabaptist churches in Germany, Anglican (Episcopalian) churches in England, Reformed churches in Switzerland and France, and Presbyterian churches in Scotland—among others. The good thing about all these churches springing up is that they could all re-form themselves into fellowships that could live out their beliefs free from the oppression and coercion of the Church of Rome. In fact, that was also good for the Roman Church, because in response to the Reformation it did a great deal to clean up its own act.

What's sad, though, is the way in which this fragmentation—necessary as it may have been at the time—split up the visible body of Christ on earth. All these churches have continued to divide again and again, often over fairly minor differences. This has resulted in a vast array of churches, making well-meaning seekers and new Christians scratch their heads in bewilderment. Which is the real church? Which one should I join? Which one really teaches and lives what the Bible says? In fact, most of them do. But each church brings its own unique emphasis.

The Birth of the Reformed Churches

The *Reformed Churches* formed one branch of the Protestant churches that broke from the Roman Catholic Church of that day. They began in the sixteenth century in Switzerland

FAST FORWARD

For a quick and easy way to visualize the church neighborhood as it has developed, take a peek at Cornelius Plantinga's diagram in Appendix A.

under the leadership of Ulrich Zwingli and John Calvin. Calvin's teachings became the dominant and leading force in these churches as they spread across Europe, particularly to France, the Netherlands, Scotland, and, by the eighteenth century, to North America, Africa, Hungary, Indonesia, and many other parts of the globe.

John Calvin was born in Noyon, France, in 1509. Educated in the humanities, he earned his academic stripes summa cum laude at age twenty-four. Inspired by the teachings of reformers like Martin Luther, Calvin took up serious study of the Bible. His education and his knowledge of Greek and Hebrew gave him access to what for most people remained a hidden book. His study of the Bible prompted him to write commentaries on almost every book of Scripture. He never did tackle the book of Revelation, which may have been wise on his part, given the endless variety of interpretations that generate so much more heat than light today. He also wrote a fabulous summary of biblical teaching entitled *The Institutes of the Christian Religion.* Calvin's works still serve as excellent resources for studying God's Word. In fact, the *Institutes* have just been translated and published in Russian and are enjoying an enthusiastic response.

Because he was persecuted by the Roman Church, Calvin had to flee France. He was drafted by another Reformer, Guillaume Farel, to support the Protestant cause in Geneva, Switzerland. There Calvin became an active preacher, teacher, leader, and proponent of Reformation teachings. While in many ways a child of his age, Calvin made a tremendous contribution to helping us understand the Bible and the faith to which it calls us. We'll explore more of his teachings when we turn to the distinctive beliefs of the Reformed/Presbyterian churches.

Reformed teaching was introduced to Scotland by John Knox, who was initially influenced by the Lutheran stream of the Reformation. His teacher, Patrick Hamilton, was burned to death for his faith, and Knox himself was captured by the French and forced into hard labor as a galley slave. Once freed, he studied with Calvin in Geneva, returning to Scotland in 1559. In spite of stiff opposition from both church and state, Knox succeeded in establishing what came to be known as the Presbyterian Church.

So What's the Difference?

How did Calvin get along with other church leaders of his day? Opposing Roman Catholic teachings of the time, he *agreed* with the other Reformers that

- Salvation is by grace alone through faith, and not by our own good works.

- The Bible alone is the authoritative Word of God for our lives—not church tradition or what church leaders say.

- *All* believers are priests of God, anointed in Christ to serve him always, everywhere, in all they do.

- God gave us two sacraments, baptism and communion, which are signs and seals of God's promises.

- A clergy's blessing of the communion bread and wine do *not* really turn them into the actual body and blood of Christ.

- The original sinful condition in which we are born as well as our actual sins are all fully washed away by Christ's one sacrifice on the cross.

- Prayer should be directed to God alone, not to saints or to Mary. In fact, all believers are both sinners needing God's constant forgiveness and saints whom the Holy Spirit is already remaking to be like Jesus.

So what were some of the differences that have kept the followers of these Reformers in separate denominations ever since? Here are a few:

- Calvin differed with Luther on how Christ is present in the Lord's Supper. Calvin taught that Jesus was not physically present but was spiritually present through the work of the Holy Spirit in believers' hearts. Luther taught that Christ was in some sense still physically present in the bread and wine. Calvin also had a different view of how the kingdom of God actually operates in this present world. And Calvin placed more emphasis on how we should live *as a result of God's grace* while Luther placed more emphasis on continually experiencing that grace itself.

- Calvin differed with Zwingli on the Lord's Supper. Calvin taught that in communion Jesus actively participates. Jesus is our host who actually gives us his grace through the operation of the Holy Spirit. Zwingli taught

FAST FORWARD

Don't worry if this section sounds like Greek to you. Go ahead and skip it if it does. Later we'll have a chance to examine these teachings at our leisure. For now it's important to realize that the Reformers agreed on the really important issues, like the fact that God saves us out of sheer mercy and grace because we cannot and should not try to save ourselves. The disagreements between Reformers were relatively minor. But they were significant enough to keep them from forming a single, unified Protestant church. A pity!

that communion was our own doing—our remembering what Jesus did for us on the cross.

- Calvin differed with the Anabaptists on the role of civil government. Calvin saw government as a necessary agent of God to which Christians had to submit and which they had to actively support. The Anabaptists taught that civil government was only for non-Christians and that those within the kingdom of God had to separate themselves from civil society. Calvin also maintained the tradition of infant baptism, a practice rejected by the Anabaptists in favor of believer's baptism.

- Calvin differed with the Anglicans/Episcopalians on many of the same points as he did with the Church of Rome. Anglicanism broke with the corrupt leadership of the Roman Church but retained many of its teachings.

Pros and Cons

Before he went to the cross to earn our salvation, Jesus prayed to his Father:

> "My prayer is not for them alone. I pray also for those who will believe in me through their message, that all of them may be one, Father, just as you are in me and I am in you. May they also be in us so that the world may believe that you have sent me."
>
> —John 17:20-21

Clearly Jesus wanted the church to be one unified fellowship around the whole world. But through these two millennia the church has

WORD ALERT

Salvation means the forgiveness of our sins and the resulting new and everlasting relationship we may enjoy with God and each other in a cleaned-up, renewed world. *Grace* means the undeserved goodness and love of God by which God gives us what we cannot earn for ourselves: salvation.

been fractured into different groups—groups that often tear each other apart over relatively unimportant things. There's no denying that the Reformation contributed to this fragmentation. So was it good or was it bad that it happened?

Thoughtful Reformed Christians would probably answer that question by saying it was both. It was bad that the Reformation had to break up the visible unity of the church. But it was good that it did so because the church in those days had gone so far astray. Luther, Calvin, Knox, and Zwingli never wanted to break up the body of Christ. That's why we call them "Reformers." They wanted to stay in the church. They urgently tried to get the Church of Rome to *re-form*, to become obedient again to the Word of God. That was their aim—not to establish their own brand of Christianity. But they ran out of choices when the church leaders of their day stubbornly refused to budge and persecuted them ruthlessly. The Reformers *had* to break from the existing church. Notice in the verse above how Jesus prays not only for unity but also asks that believers will remain in God. When the church drifted away from God, the Reformers saw no option but to return to the straight and narrow as commanded by Scripture, even when it meant breaking ranks with the Roman Catholic Church.

Where does that leave us? We need to stay true to the teaching of Scripture. That's the only way we can stay in Christ. However, we should always, always be looking for opportunities to join with other Christians. We should work with them even if our differences will not allow us, yet, to routinely worship with them. We need to keep reaching out to each other as we continue to reach for our Bibles. We may not always agree on doctrine or on how to worship. But there's plenty we can agree on that God wants us to do in this impoverished, sin-wracked world. So let's join efforts and do what needs doing together. Let's make our own unique contribution to God's mission, using the particular gifts God's Spirit has given us. That way we may be the hands and feet and voice of our Savior for those who need to share in his goodness. Then we'll still be functioning as Christ's body. And the world will experience God's reconciling love.

As Reformed Christians we want to keep praying both of these: "Lord, keep us obediently in you" and "Lord, make us one." And to the best of our ability we'll need to work at both, right along with our Roman Catholic, Pentecostal, and Baptist sisters and brothers.

Person to Person

Reformed teaching matters to flesh-and-blood people in real-life circumstances and situations. Here's the first of three stories of people who have adopted the Reformed faith as their own. In telling what they most value about it, they help us to rediscover and celebrate its riches for ourselves. You'll find the other two stories in the next chapters.

My spiritual identity and affection for Reformed theology is due to the faithfulness of my parents. My parents were immigrants from China who came to America in the late 1940s with the intention of returning home after their studies. War and revolution unexpectedly preempted a return, so I was raised an "ABC" (American-born Chinese) in New York City.

Living in Queens at the crossroads between American and Chinese culture provided interesting tensions. Do I learn Mandarin or play Little League baseball? What role models do I look up to—Bruce Lee or Mickey Mantle? Visiting Hebrew school with neighbors during the day and studying the Heidelberg Catechism with my family at night was not uncommon. Fortunately, my church—a Chinese ministry located in a predominantly Jewish neighborhood—provided a safe spiritual haven from secular society.

The contrast in cultures puzzled me and led me to question why God made things this way. Moreover, my family and church life overlapped in such a way that it was difficult to tell where one began and the other ended. Theological reflection seemed to dominate every sphere of our lives. It dominated conversations at breakfast, youth outings, visits to Yankee Stadium, and mundane drives through the Holland Tunnel. My parents taught me that faith must be lived and not merely assented to. They believed that to be Reformed was a matter of doing rather than merely adhering to a set of beliefs. Intellectual nonconformity was essential since God had endowed us with the capacity for critical reflection. New York City provided a ready context to test Christian ideas about faith, culture, and ethnic identity.

Despite my Christian upbringing and intense church life, I did not yet personally grasp the deep reality of God's self-revelation. It was not until a late winter afternoon while reading the *Collected Writings of John Murray* that I personally grasped the weight of my fallen condition, my redemption through faith in Jesus Christ, and the wisdom of Reformed theology. It was a real challenge to trudge through Murray's dry treatise on systematic theology. But in a strangely providential way it brought tears to my eyes. To my amazement I couldn't hold back my tears as what I had learned as a youth sprang back into my life with profound personal meaning. Although Murray was discussing the nuances of "effectual calling," what he was clearly telling me was that "Jesus loves me, this I know, for the Bible tells me so." It dawned on me that special afternoon that all along Reformed theology had simply taken this basic truth and connected it to every sphere of life. Today, knowledge of this plain yet comprehensive truth stills brings me to tears of awe, appreciation, and ecstasy.

—Peter Szto

Peter Szto works for the office of race relations for the Christian Reformed Church as the regional staff person for the Midwest and East Coast.

Points to Ponder

1. Were the Reformers right in breaking with the Church of Rome? Were the issues important enough?

2. What should I do if I disagree with what my church teaches or does?

3. Should the Reformers have compromised with each other and formed only one single Reformation church?

4. Should we work toward uniting with other churches, or would that draw us too far away from obedience to God? What can we do to work toward unity?

CHAPTER 2

God's in Charge

What are the teachings that Reformed types hold dear? Actually, they are nothing more and nothing less than key teachings of the Bible itself. So it's no surprise that many Reformed teachings are shared by many other Christians as well. But because of the way Reformed Christians interpret the Bible, we emphasize some biblical teachings more strongly than other Christians do.

Here's a handy way to remember the distinctive teachings of Reformed and Presbyterian churches. Reformed Christians like to first *see* what God does before seeing what we ourselves can and ought to do in response. So let's see what God does for us. God

- Controls
- Communicates
- Confirms
- Cleanses
- Claims

In the rest of this chapter and in the next, let's take a quick glance at these five highlights of Reformed teaching. They really come as a package deal. Taken together they emphasize the dynamic, saving work of our all-powerful, loving

God. The Bible reassures us that our good God will certainly renew the whole world. That includes us—despite our own inability and weakness. We can count on God! That's the heart of the Reformed emphasis. Reformed teaching points us away from our own efforts because those cannot make us right with God. Our efforts cannot rebuild God's broken world or even our own broken lives. But they don't have to. Reformed teaching points us to what God does and what God promises to do for us, in us, and through us that we cannot do for or by ourselves. And God has never broken a promise yet. Believing in God's faithfulness gives us a deep security and confidence. This deeply felt confidence and assurance is, perhaps, the most precious contribution of the Reformed tradition to the Christian church as a whole.

God Controls

Ever lie awake at night worrying whether or not you're really right with God? Have you committed too many sins? Have you done enough good to balance the scales? Is your faith strong enough to hang in there for a lifetime? Will Judgment Day drag you before an angry God who shakes his head in bitter disappointment at your performance and who sentences you to an eternity of indescribable suffering in hell?

If you have worried about that . . . congratulations! It's a sure sign that God's Holy Spirit is working in your heart, prodding you to ask the really important questions in life.

So how would the Bible answer your questions? Like this:

- No, you're *not* right with God. You're a sinner, and despite all your best efforts you're only digging yourself in deeper every day (Romans 3:10-12).

- Yes, you *have* committed too many sins, and even a single sin is enough for you to deserve the fate you visualize in your worst nightmare (Ephesians 5:5-6).

- No, you *haven't* done enough good to balance the scales. You can't begin to make up for even a single sin even if your best works were acceptable to God—which they aren't (Isaiah 64:6-7).

- No, your faith *isn't* nearly strong enough to see you through—not without God's help. Jesus had a disciple by the name of Peter. Peter had more faith than most of us. He accepted Jesus' invitation and stepped out of a boat and walked on water in the middle of a horrible storm. Would you risk that? Yet Peter's faith wasn't strong enough. It made him waver. He would have drowned if Jesus hadn't reached out his hand and rescued him. Later Peter denied his Lord three times and would have stuck to fishing if Jesus hadn't yanked him back into the kingdom of God. If even Peter's faith wasn't strong enough to see him through, ours isn't either. But, praise God, it doesn't have to be . . . Jesus is power-ful enough to save even "little-faiths" like Peter and you and me (Matthew 14:31).

- No, Judgment Day will *not* place you before an angry God who will condemn you to hell. That's what you deserve. But it's not what you'll get. Believe in him and you'll find Jesus, your own defense lawyer, on the judge's bench! You'll be given a full pardon because God did for you what you cannot do for yourself—he justified you, making you right with him. And he'll hang onto you even when your own faith falters. Promise! Need proof? Get it straight from the Good Shepherd's mouth: "I give them eternal life, and they shall never perish; no one can snatch them out of my hand" (John 10:18).

In a nutshell, that's what the Reformed churches emphasize. God is in control. God does for us what we cannot do for ourselves. If God had not chosen us first, we would never have chosen him. If God did not give us saving faith through the Holy Spirit and his Word, we would never be able to conjure up that faith in and of ourselves. Saving faith is a precious gift of God to us. If God did not save us, nobody else could save us, certainly not ourselves. If God did not protect us every day, the hostile powers of darkness would steal our souls and our lives in a split second. Because God is in control over everything I can be sure I'm right with him—not because I'm strong enough or good enough. If we belong to God, nothing—not even our own doubts, failures, and dumb moves—can snatch us from our Savior's grip. He's got the whole world in his hand—and that includes us.

This emphasis on God's sovereignty threads its way through a lot of biblical teachings that Reformed believers hold dear:

- Salvation is by God's grace alone, not by our works (Ephesians 2:8).

- We are saved by faith alone, which is itself God's gift to us, not our own achievement (Ephesians 2:8).

- God chooses us before we can choose for God—we're all adopted children (John 3:3-5; Romans 8:28-30).

- God makes a covenant with us to be our God, and we shall be God's people. But every covenant has two parts. We have to live up to our part of the agreement. But we can't. We're too weak. So God not only upholds his end of that covenant but upholds our end as well. God sent us Jesus to be our perfect representative to uphold the agreement on our behalf (Matthew 26:27-29). And God sends us the Holy Spirit to enable us to begin living up to it personally as well (John 14:16-17).

- Infants should be baptized as well as adults who come to faith. In baptism God approaches us first, taking the initiative. The covenant promises are extended to us *before* we choose either to accept or reject its terms. So we should not wait until our children reach the age of consent (Acts 2:39). They become members of God's family at the same time they become members of ours. They become citizens of God's kingdom at the same time they become citizens of our country.

FACTOID

Although Calvin himself had nothing to do with it, his distinctive teachings on God's sovereignty are often summarized by the acronym TULIP. TULIP stands for

- *Total Depravity*—sin has so corrupted our nature that we cannot save ourselves or even seek out God on our own.

- *Unconditional Election*—God adopts us as children not because we are more deserving than others but only out of God's own sovereign love for us.

- *Limited Atonement*—while Jesus' death on the cross was sufficient to cover the sins of the whole world, the benefits of his death are applied only to those whom God has chosen.

- *Irresistible Grace*—like infants who are adopted, our heavenly Father's gracious action of making us part of the family is irresistible.

- *Preservation of the Saints*—our Father in heaven will never abandon his children. When we belong to God no one, not even the devil

25

himself, will ever be able to steal us away.

In *F.A.I.T.H. Unfolded* (available from Faith Alive Christian Resources, 1-800-333-8300), Jim Oosterhouse proposes an acronym that I think communicates these teachings more clearly, effectively, and biblically than TULIP:

- **F**allen Humankind
- **A**dopted by God
- **I**ntentional Atonement
- **T**ransformed by the Spirit
- **H**eld by God

- We have assurance that we belong to God and that we will live with him forever, not because we have confidence in ourselves, but because we have confidence in our heavenly Father. God would never *think* of losing the children he's adopted (Hosea 11:1-11). Would you?

God Communicates
The Truth of the Bible Confirmed

OK. So you're lying awake again and this time you worry about whether you've got the right religion. After all, there are hundreds of religions and hundreds of books that claim to have the truth. How do you know you're not terribly mistaken in your Christian beliefs?

Congratulations again. The Spirit is *really* stirring in your heart now! Never be afraid of those honest questions. They're not the devil's work. They're God's work, tempering your faith, making it grow strong and firm and solid. You've raised a good question, and Paul answers it in 1 Corinthians 15:

> And if Christ has not been raised, your faith is futile; you are still in your sins. Then those also who have fallen asleep in Christ are lost. If only for this life we have hope in Christ, we are to be pitied more than all men.
>
> But Christ has indeed been raised from the dead, the firstfruits of those who have fallen asleep.
>
> —1 Corinthians 15:17-20

Jesus and the apostles he personally instructed and appointed clearly confirm for us that the Bible is the reliable Word of God. How can we be so sure?

Jesus *proved* it. He fulfilled what the Old Testament promised. He proved he was the Son of God, our Savior and Lord, as the New Testament announces. How? He died and rose again from the dead! Pretty good evidence, don't you think? You try doing that! Jesus provided the rock-solid historical evidence that no other religious book or leader has ever duplicated.

Jesus claims that he is God the Son come to give us eternal life. He doesn't just promise it. He proves it so clearly that we can safely bet our soul's eternal salvation on it. Before a great many witnesses he lets himself be brutally murdered and buried in a rich man's grave. And then he reappears in the flesh, very much alive. He goes eyeball to eyeball with his disciples and with more than five hundred other witnesses. He even lets a doubting Thomas physically probe and test the nail wounds in his hands and the scar in his side (John 20:28) to prove he's not just a phantom, a magician's trick, or a pious dream.

Is Jesus' resurrection from the dead an outrageous claim made by grieving disciples? Not a chance! It would have been ever so simple at the time the New Testament was written to discredit this historical claim. The naysayers needed only to produce Jesus' corpse. They didn't. They couldn't! Jesus had undeniably risen from the dead. He proved resurrections can and do happen. He proved we can trust God to give us eternal life. He got eternal life first and brought it back to us to show it and tell it. Through his death and resurrection Jesus firmly anchors the reliability of the Bible on the bedrock of history.

The Testimony of the Spirit

So maybe the Bible does give solid evidence that it is the reliable Word of God. But how does its message penetrate into my heart and soul? How does it convince me and assure me in the depth of my being? Calvin's prescription is simple. Read it! Read the Bible with an open mind, and the Holy Spirit will convince you over and over again that it is the true, solid, reliable Word of God. As it speaks to you and witnesses to the story of Jesus and his love for us, the Spirit will testify to its reliability and convince you of its truthfulness. Oh, and while you're at it, Calvin suggests, stop counting organ pipes or wall tiles during worship, and pay some attention to the sermon. The Holy Spirit uses preaching to feed our faith if and when that preaching faithfully explains and applies God's Word to our lives. Then pay attention as well when there's a baptism or when you participate in the Lord's Supper. Through those sacraments the Holy Spirit not only uses words to apply God's Word, but actions as well.

So Jesus Christ and the apostles confirm the Bible's claims for itself. And the Holy Spirit testifies to its truth within our hearts as we read it, hear it, and celebrate it. But what exactly *does* the Bible claim for itself? We'd better let the Bible speak for itself:

> For prophecy never had its origin in the will of man, but men spoke from

God as they were carried along by the
Holy Spirit.

—2 Peter 1:21

All Scripture is God-breathed and is
useful for teaching, rebuking, correct-
ing and training in righteousness, so
that the man of God may be thor-
oughly equipped for every good work.

—2 Timothy 3:16-17

Reformed Christians take seriously the Bible's
own claims for itself: the Bible alone is the saving Word of God that reliably tells us what to
believe and how to live.

A High View of Scripture

What else does the Reformed faith contribute to
wider Christianity in its view of Scripture?

- The Bible is *infallible*, which means "unfailing." It is completely reliable, so we can fully
  trust it to guide us in our beliefs and our life.

- The Bible is *sufficiently clear* so that untrained
  believers can understand its message well
  enough to be saved and to grow in their faith
  by reading it. While theologians and Bible
  scholars may be helpful in teaching us more
  about the Bible, we're not dependent on
  them. Personal and family Bible reading,
  study, and meditation are important disci-
  plines for all of us—and they bring rich
  rewards.

- The Bible alone is our *rule*—only teachings
  clearly found in the Bible, not those added by

church leaders or church tradition, may guide us in what to believe and how to live. Of course, where leaders and tradition faithfully point us to Scripture itself, they can be very useful to us—think of parents, teachers, pastors, and good Christian friends (including those on your bookshelf!). But they all must stick with and be corrected by what Scripture itself clearly teaches.

- The Bible needs to be carefully *interpreted.* God only communicates to us through the Bible when we understand it correctly. Calvin didn't write over twenty commentaries on the Bible because he had nothing else to do. He realized how important it was to understand what the Bible writers intended to say in their time and how they (and the Holy Spirit) would have wanted us to apply their message today. When we misunderstand the Bible's intent, we're not hearing God's Word but rather imposing our own views, or the views of others, on it.

- The way to understand the Bible properly is to interpret it within its *context.* Calvin used a grammatical-historical interpretation. That simply means that he tried to understand the actual meaning of the words and the historical situation in which the words were spoken and written down. Calvin followed Jesus' own approach to interpreting the Bible. On the way to Emmaus the risen Jesus walks along with the two travelers, and "beginning with Moses and all the Prophets, he explained to them what was said in all the Scriptures concerning himself" (Luke 24:27). All the stories of the Bible contribute to its one overarching message that's summarized for us in John 3:16: "For God so loved the world that he gave his one and only Son, that whoever believes in him shall not perish but have eternal life." Unless we put that connection front and center in every Bible story we tell, we have not fully heard the voice of God.

Here's a simple example of how to distinguish a Reformed understanding of Scripture from that of, say, an often-used moralistic one. Take the story of God's conversation and subsequent dealings with Abraham recorded in Genesis 12 and beyond. A moralistic interpretation would tell the story like any one of Aesop's fables. God commanded Abraham to leave his country and go to another country of God's choosing. Abraham obeyed God, so God rewarded Abraham. The moral of the story: we should be like Abraham and obey God.

The Reformed perspective on this story would not deny the importance of obeying God but would put the emphasis very differently. It would find the heart of the story in God's promise to Abraham to make Abraham into a great nation through whom all the nations of the earth would be blessed. It would connect that story with the way in which God began to fulfill that promise as Abraham traveled to the Promised Land. It would then hasten on to show how God continued to fulfill that promise to Abraham by sending Jesus. It would then tell us the good news of how, in Christ, God continues to fulfill the promise by including people from all over the world as Abraham's heirs—us too! The heart of the story (as that of every Bible story) focuses on what God does. It connects that story to the grand story of Jesus and his love. And it brings it home to us in the context of our present place in the history of God's redemption. It is through Christ that God fulfills the promise made to Abraham. And by faith, we too are part of and take part in that redemption. That's why this way of interpreting Scripture is often called a "redemptive-historical" approach.

It takes some effort to get beyond Aesop. But the thrill of new, unfolding vistas of biblical exploration and meaning make it more than worth it!

Let's leave it there for now, concluding our exploration of the first two "C"s of Reformed teaching: God controls and God communicates. In the next chapter we'll survey three more.

Person to Person

I was born and raised in central Harlem in New York City. As a teenager, I was introduced to the Reformed faith by a neighbor who attended a Reformed church down the street. I found the congregation to be friendly, gracious, and supportive of my educational pursuits. Since my parents had died during my childhood, members of this church became a surrogate family for me and brought some stability to my life.

Although I was initially attracted by the church's hospitality, I later developed much respect for the minister and the preaching. In contrast to the unquestioned, charismatic authority figures I had observed in other churches, this pastor was unassuming and approachable. The central authority in the congregation resided with the church council. The sermons were less emotional, more rooted in the biblical text, and more theologically instructive than those I had heard in other churches.

Over time I began to understand the importance of the Holy Spirit's work in the Christian life; it was not I who chose to believe, but the Holy Spirit who led me to the Savior, Jesus Christ. The Spirit gave me a deep assurance that God graciously grants me eternal salvation, regardless of my efforts, material possessions, or lack thereof.

The church challenges me to integrate my Christian faith into my daily activities, vocation, and interpersonal relationships. My daily Christian behavior and attitude are more important than pious words and external appearance on Sunday. I still have much to learn about the Christian faith. But I have come to appreciate this teaching of the Reformed faith: I am sinful, and only by God's grace was I rescued from a life of despair and granted eternal life through faith in Jesus Christ.

—Barbara Bradley Feenstra

Barbara Bradley Feenstra is a physician, wife, and mother of three daughters.

Points to Ponder

1. If God is in control of everything, why do so many bad things happen? Is that God's fault? Will it always be like this?

2. If it's true that my good works don't save me, why do I—and should I—still do them?

3. Why should we believe what the Bible says?

4. Why is there so much in the Bible that's hard to understand and that seems so irrelevant to my circumstances?

5. What's the best method for daily Bible reading?

- "Poke and hope"—open the Bible any old place, hit the page with your pen, and read the chapter it falls on.
- "Seek and thou shalt find"—look up your favorite passages and read them over and over and over again.
- "Cover to cover to cover till doomsday"—read the whole Bible from Genesis to Revelation—over and over again.
- "Pick the flowers"—read a little of this, a little of that . . . a little here, a little there . . .
- "Guided tour"—read only those pieces of the Bible mentioned in devotionals.
- "Hop, skip, and jump"—read . . . whatever!
- "Reader's book club"—picking out and reading one whole book of the Bible at a time.
- "Round tuit"—you know you should, but you never get a "round tuit"

6. What passage or story from Scripture has come to be especially meaningful for you personally?

CHAPTER 3

God Claims It All

God Confirms

A number of years back a couple stopped by my office with an urgent request. They were grief-stricken from the sudden loss to crib death of their three-month-old baby. They were not members of my church, they said. But they wondered if I, as a pastor, could find it in my heart to baptize their dead infant. The loss of their child was incredibly painful to them. But even more painful was the thought that their dearly loved baby daughter might miss out on eternal life because they had neglected to get her baptized.

I was powerless to heal the hurt of their grievous loss. But I could pass on to them some biblical comfort about the eternal well-being of their baby. The fact that they did not have their daughter baptized did not in any way, shape, or form determine the eternal destination of their child. I could assure them that by means of their faith in Jesus their child was forever sheltered and safe in the arms of our loving Good Shepherd.

Did I let them off the hook too easily?

Absolutely not!

FASTFORWARD

Up to speed on the sacraments and eager to see what's next? Drop to the "God Cleanses" section. But before you do, remember that the Reformed position on the sacraments takes a mediating position between the Roman Catholic view and the Anabaptist and Zwinglian view. If you're not sure how, you may want to press "play" here instead.

The Reformed faith emphasizes that baptism and communion are signs and seals of God's promises. They are not those promises themselves.

There are churches that teach that the sacraments are necessary for salvation—forego baptism or communion and you cannot go to heaven. Baptism, they teach, is the only way you become God's child. Communion is the only way in which you receive salvation.

Reformed Christians don't buy that argument. The sacraments are God-given confirmations of God's deeds, not the deeds themselves.

Here's an example. You use your slow-as-molasses computer to go online and order up a faster one. You punch in your charge-card number, and the company duly acknowledges the deal by e-mailing you a confirmation. You download it. Suddenly you come to your senses and decide you shouldn't buy another computer because you really can't afford it. So you go to your in-basket, open up the confirmation notice, and blast it into cyberspace. There. That's that. No more computer purchase.

Um . . . not so fast. The confirmation isn't the deal itself. The confirmation reminded and reassured you that the transaction happened. But confirmation is only confirmation. Deleting it doesn't undo the deal at all. You'd better keep an eye out for that delivery truck—and your credit card balance as well.

That's the case with the sacraments of baptism and Lord's Supper. They are invaluable ways by

which God makes us see and touch and taste
what God has really promised to do for us. That
makes them important ways by which our faith
can grow. But they are not the actions themselves. Were the church to refuse to administer
these sacraments, people could still be saved all
the same. God allows us to spread the gospel
and to confirm it through the sacraments. But
our Lord is still in charge. Salvation is Christ's
work. And he'll portion it out as he sees fit, even
if we fail to do our part.

Gracious Acts of God

Let's apply this concept to the couple in my
office. They neglected to have their child baptized. That was too bad for them. They deprived
themselves of a terrific comfort that might have
reassured them in their grief. But baptism would
not have washed away the sin of their child.
Only Jesus Christ, who died on the cross two
thousand years ago, could do that. Through
Jesus' death God saved their child. And through
their faith God applied the cleansing merit of
Christ's death to their baby (Acts 2:39; 1 Corinthians 7:14). Sacrament or no sacrament, God
remains faithful to his Word.

The same applies to the Lord's Supper. The
Reformed faith teaches that the bread and wine
(or juice) do not actually turn into the body and
blood of Christ. Jesus' blood was shed for us
once and for all on Calvary. No further sacrificing of his body or shedding of his blood needs
to be done. So at the Lord's Supper Jesus is not
bodily present with us. But Jesus *is* really with us
through the Spirit working in our hearts. Jesus is
our host, feeding our faith and allowing us to
share in his grace. But he remains bodily up in

heaven. Through the Lord's Supper Jesus confirms for us what happened so long ago. Through the sacrament we not only see Christ's saving grace—we can touch it, taste it, and eat and drink it.

Reformed/Presbyterian types speak of two different ways in which God strengthens our faith through the sacraments:

- Sacraments are *signs* and *symbols* that demonstrate a reality that we cannot yet see with our eyes: God's salvation extended to us through Jesus' death and resurrection.

- Sacraments are *seals* which confirm that we belong to God.

A seal is the equivalent of a signature. In the old days you would prove a document was yours by imprinting your unique seal into wax that you dripped onto the paper. Similarly, when we place our signature on a document we do more than just attach some kind of mark or symbol. We make it our own! By signing our name we confirm that we are responsible for fulfilling what we agreed to do. Anyone can call us on it. Our signature ties us to what we put in the document.

It's the same with the sacraments. Through them we receive the guarantee that God's promises belong to us personally. Here, in my baptism, Father, Son, and Holy Spirit write their signature in water on my forehead. That makes me sure that I really belong to God's family. And here, in communion, my Savior lets me chew on the rich salvation he earned for me by sacrificing his own body and blood. Jesus applies his saving work to me so really and truly that I can touch it, feel it, and taste it!

There's one other twist to the Reformed understanding of the sacraments. Why do we identify only two sacraments when other Christian churches identify up to seven? Because these signs and seals of God's promises are the only two that Jesus specifically commanded us to celebrate. That's what the Bible says. And as we saw earlier, the Bible should be our only authority on such things.

God Cleanses

Renewed

A while back my son had the misfortune of making the family sedan about a foot shorter than it was supposed to be. He readily convinced the investigating officer (and me, as I drove up) that it wasn't his fault and that there was nothing he could have done to prevent the collision. The officer agreed. There would be no fine. My son was *justified*—he was deemed to be in compliance with the law.

That was a relief to both my son and me. The officer got back in the cruiser and disappeared over the hill. Soon, though, we were absorbed in checking out the damage, determining if the car was still drivable, and how we might get it fixed. My son's being justified with respect to the law kept him from getting punished. But it did nothing at all to put the car back together. It was still a wreck. It needed skilled hands, lots of elbow grease, and tons of money to restore it to its original condition.

SO WHAT

When my life gets rough and I'm only focused on the here and now, I often turn a blind eye to God. But then the sacraments pull me right back to the center of what my life is all about. In a few simple gestures they remind me of the *big* picture. That's immensely comforting and gives me new energy and hope. I'm ready to let God lead me on my next step of faith.

FACTOID

The Roman Catholic Church, for example, identifies seven sacraments: baptism, confirmation, absolution, communion, marriage, ordination, and last rites. Reformed churches have their own rites resembling all of these. But apart from baptism and communion, Reformed churches don't consider these acts sacraments.

That's how it is with our sins as well. When we sin, we ruin our relationship to God and to each other. And we make a horrible mess of God's world. We don't do ourselves any favors either—"for the wages of sin is death" (Romans 6:23). And the worst of it is that, above and beyond those consequences of our sin, our disobedience makes us guilty before God's law as well. We become liable to the penalty of spending eternity banished from God's holy and perfect presence.

The good news the Bible brings us is that Jesus died for our sins. Throughout his life, and especially on Calvary, he bore the punishment and penalty that we deserve for our sin. Through his willing sacrifice he has removed our guilt before God's law. Believers are *justified*, made right, before God. We were justified in a way different than my son in the nasty business of the car accident, of course. He was justified because he didn't do anything wrong, while we are justified in spite of the fact that we have done lots of wrong.

But, as in my son's case, that's only part of the story! Being justified does not magically take away all the consequences of our evil deeds. My car still needed the body shop. Similarly, we need God to renew us and restore us—to make us as good and loving and righteous and pure and obedient as Jesus is (and Adam once was). We do not only need to be *justified*, we also need to be *sanctified*. That work of restoring us, making us new creatures who rightly image God, is also God's work. God sent the Holy Spirit to accomplish that task. How does the Spirit do that? In lots of ways:

WORD ALERT

Sanctified means "washed clean." The word is often used for the ritual washing the priests underwent before they were allowed to offer up the sacrifices devoted to God.

- giving us the Bible
- giving us true faith
- joining us to the church
- giving us spiritual gifts we can share
- helping us to pray
- giving us self-control and love so we can do God's will
- giving us the fruit of the Spirit
- giving us hope for the future
- empowering us to join in God's mission of evangelizing the world
- giving us new life in Christ

While the Spirit has already begun to renew us in Christ, there are two tasks that won't be completed until later. The Spirit will fully take away our sinful nature (which is still, regrettably, a part of us) when we die. And the Spirit will raise us up from the dead on Judgment Day. Then we shall be perfect as God is perfect.

Notice that Reformed teaching emphasizes both justification and sanctification as saving works of God. In Jesus God makes us right with him. Through the Holy Spirit God makes us alright. Some Christian traditions stress only the first of these, concentrating on the good news that Jesus saves sinners. But the Reformed faith puts equal stress on the work of the Holy Spirit—how the Spirit empowers us to live a new life of loving, obedient service to God, to God's people, and to the world.

Such a new life of discipleship to Jesus is not our attempt to make ourselves right with God. Remember, Jesus alone makes us right with God. But our new life is the inevitable result of what Jesus has done for us. He took away our

41

sin and he gave us his Spirit. And the Holy Spirit, living in our hearts, fills us with gratitude for what God has done for us, and with an eager longing to live as God's joyful, loving children. We pray and we work hard to please God because God has already saved us and made us his children. We don't need to earn our salvation. We're free to live it out every day anew.

Born Again and Learning to Live

Reformed Christians sometimes don't know what to say when they're asked if they are "born-again Christians." Some will say no, because they mistakenly equate the label "born again" with the notion of a "second blessing" or an additional outpouring of God's Spirit that allows you to do things like speak in tongues or heal people. However, the Reformed faith doesn't make a separation between "first-class" and "economy-fare" Christians. Either you're a believer, and therefore Spirit-filled, or you're not a believer.

Other Reformed Christians might answer, "Yes, of course I'm a born-again Christian—what other kind is there?" That might sound a bit snooty, but it points to another Reformed distinctive.

Reformed teaching uses two key words to describe the cleansing work of God's Spirit in our lives. And it defines those words very carefully.

The first is the word *regeneration,* or, more simply, *rebirth.* Those words explain why Reformed Christians consider themselves and *all* believers "born-again Christians." They don't mean that they have some special anointing of the Holy Spirit above and beyond what all Christ-believers have. They mean that the Holy Spirit makes believers alive spiritually even though they are dead in their own sins. They echo the words of Jesus in John 3:5: "I tell you the truth, no one can enter the kingdom of God unless he is born of water and the Spirit." Our rebirth occurs when the Holy Spirit plants saving faith into our hearts. Our faith is not born from our own work—just like our first birth wasn't our own doing—but from God's work in us. Through rebirth God makes us alive spiritually by giving us faith.

But being born is just the start. A healthy baby doesn't just sit passively and idly by because she has been born. She spends a great deal of effort learning to live this life that she has been given. Learning to eat and to talk and to crawl and to walk takes a lot of hard work. She needs persistence too, because the failures are many.

The Reformed faith emphasizes the parallel with our spiritual life as well. Once we are given rebirth through God's Spirit we haven't arrived. In fact, we've just begun our spiritual journey. It'll take time to find our "spiritual legs" and to learn the language of faith. We'll have to learn to live all over again. In the process we'll make lots of mistakes. We'll slide back into our old ways time and time again. *Conversion*—the second term we use in this context—is a lifelong process, a constant discipline of putting off our sinful and evil ways and learning to live as loving, obedient children of God and as faithful disciples of Jesus.

FACTOID

Reformed Christians disagree on such things as speaking in tongues, a second blessing, miraculous healing, and driving out demons. Some argue that these things were done by Jesus and the apostles to confirm their preaching, and that such signs are no longer needed in our time because we have the confirmation of Scripture, so now the Spirit no longer provides them. Others argue that the Bible nowhere teaches that these gifts would be phased out and so they see them as continuing ways the Spirit uses to spread the good Word. These people are often identified as "charismatics," which means they believe that the Spirit still provides these "special gifts." So don't assume that no Reformed folks are charismatics—or that all of them are.

Some conversions are dramatic. Think of Paul on the road to Damascus. Your own conversion may have been dramatic as well. You came to a point in your life where Jesus took you by the collar and spun you around 180 degrees. You were headed for hell and now you're headed toward God. Praise the Lord!

Other conversions happen over years, maybe even decades. Think of Timothy, who grew up in a Christian home. He could probably never identify the exact time that God turned his life around.

In either case, once you've made that crucial turn, you're not there yet. Your old self will continue to try to pull you off course again and again. You'll have to make midcourse corrections all along the way. The Christian life is one of constant, ongoing conversion—like a car that's now headed in the right direction but needs constant steering to keep it on course. The Holy Spirit will have to keep nudging us in the right direction until we're parked safely and permanently in God's completed kingdom.

God Claims

As a young teen I once tagged along with an elder from my church. We were distributing flyers around the neighborhood, inviting people to join us for Sunday worship. One crusty elderly gent took a quick glance at the leaflet I placed in his hand. He grumped, "I know you guys— you're just after my money." The elder's reply startled me. "No, we're not just after your money. We want it all—your possessions, your time, your work, your heart and soul, your body—*everything*. God deserves no less."

An honest reply, telling people right up front what the cost of discipleship really is. God gave his very own Son for us. Jesus gave us his life. The Spirit moved right into our hearts and took up permanent residence there. That kind of total commitment deserves our total response as well, body and soul.

Reformed Christianity emphasizes God's claim over all of life—personal and communal, public and private, individual and collective. That's because the Bible clearly teaches that Jesus is much more than only our Savior. Jesus is Lord of all (Philippians 2:9-11). Abraham Kuyper, a well-known Dutch Reformed politician, scholar, and preacher, put it well: "There is not an inch of all creation of which Jesus does not say, 'Mine!'"

This Reformed emphasis goes against the grain of our modern culture. We're conditioned to think that life is made up of two separate pieces: the sacred and the secular. The sacred is that part of our lives that we devote to God: our worship, our volunteer time, the money we give to church and donations we might make to charities. The secular is that part of our lives that we devote to our own well-being: making a living, possibly raising a family, participating in our society, and entertaining ourselves.

Reformed Christians fight dualism tooth and nail. They believe that God created all things. God created them all good. Not only our souls or spirits, but also our bodies, belong head, heart, hands, and toenails to our Creator. God created the stuff of this world and the complex interactions and interrelationships that we bump into daily: the environment, the marketplace, education, politics, you name it—God made it and owns it. All of creation, including our whole life, is sacred, devoted to God's glory. That is the very purpose for which everything exists.

The fact that our sinfulness got this world into its present sorry mess doesn't make the world any less God's. Our disobedience gives the devil's evil empire lots of control. But the world still belongs to God. And in Jesus Christ God is reclaiming this world, inch by inch, to restore it to its original goodness and purpose. Wherever God's people obediently work in the light of God's Word, there they reclaim this fallen creation for their Lord and build his kingdom.

This means that our daily work is holy. It's a calling—whether it's farming, office work, or the gospel ministry. Where we contribute to the development of God's creation and of society, there we're serving God. Our family life too is as much a spiritual matter as our involvement in church. How we clothe ourselves, feed ourselves, amuse ourselves—these things too are directly related to our service of God. Our world belongs to God. And so do we.

It's tough sometimes to know how we should live in this world. There's so much brokenness that we often don't know where to start. It's hard to earn a decent buck and to earn it decently. It's difficult to influence government and society in positive ways. But we need not get discouraged. Our ascended Lord will continue to grow his kingdom in this world. Like a little yeast working its way through a large clump of dough, you may not be able to see God's kingdom grow. But

WORD ALERT

The word *glory* in Scripture refers to God's greatness and splendor—those characteristics that make us (naturally) fear, praise, adore, and worship God.

WORD ALERT

The Reformers often spoke of "the priesthood of all believers" (based on I Peter 2:9). Not only clergy are God's specially chosen servants; all believers share in the special calling of being Christ's representatives on earth. We do that in different ways. Clergy do it in one way. Factory workers, nurses, and lawyers do it in other ways. But we all devote our life and our life's work to God's service. That makes all of us priests.

grow it will (Matthew 13:33)! And once Jesus returns he will restore all things, so that the whole creation once more sings one endless song of praise to God.

In the meantime we have a world to win back. Wherever we bring the good news that Jesus is Lord, the kingdom of God expands. Wherever we learn greater obedience in the way we live, relate to each other, and take care of God's world, there the kingdom grows. Wherever we raise children in God's ways, wherever we advance the cause of justice and lend a helping hand to those in need, there we see the kingdom advance. It's a big world and we're people of little strength and will. But it's a big God that leads us on. King Jesus will reclaim every inch of our world in due time. In the meantime he appoints each of us as ambassadors for that kingdom. Never thought you were that important? Well, you are!

Person to Person

I was born in Montpelier, Vermont, to a Castillian (Spanish) father and a New England Yankee mother. I spent my childhood in Barre, Vermont, where I attended school with French Canadians, Scots, Irish, Italians, Spaniards, English, and Poles, among others. We spoke English at home and Spanish when we visited my paternal grandmother. I attended a liberal Congregational church.

As a young adult I began attending my home church with more regularity. I joined the youth group, was received into full fellowship in the church, and began singing in the chancel choir. Each Sunday as I put on the choir robe and marched down the center aisle in the processional, I felt somewhat "holier." It wasn't until I began to attend Reformed Bible Institute that I began to realize my need for a personal relationship with Christ. I also began frequenting a Reformed and a Christian Reformed Church on Sunday evenings. That's how TULIP came onto my path, and I finally committed my life to Christ.

As a new Christian I soaked up everything I could get my hands on. I worked in the shoe department at a local department store. In between serving customers I read Kuyper's *Stone Lectures* on Calvinism. It was this doctrine of the sovereignty of God—of God's rule over all of life—from worship to school to selling shoes, that helped me realize I had found a home in the Reformed faith. It teaches a theology that made sense to me. The Reformed faith has truly helped me to recognize God's grace and vigilant care for me as a child of the covenant.

—Gary Teja

Gary Teja works for Christian Reformed Home Missions as the Hispanic ministry director and as a member of the executive staff for new church development.

Points to Ponder

1. Compare baptism to citizenship in your country of origin. What are some similarities? Are there differences?

2. So are *you* a born-again Christian? How can you tell? Please explain.

3. Are there people who are *justified* but who are not *sanctified?* Why or why not?

4. The Bible teaches that Jesus is Lord over all creation. Why does he wait so long to put everything right? How would you respond to this oft-quoted limerick?

> God's plan made a hopeful beginning
> But man ruined his chances by sinning.
> We trust that the story
> Will end in God's glory
> But at present the other side's winning.

5. What areas of your life still need to be claimed for Christ's kingdom? (Go ahead, take a risk, be specific.) If you're successful at that will you still have any leisure time left? Will you still have any fun?

CHAPTER 4

Reforming Day By Day

If the Reformed teachings are worth anything then they have to make a difference in the way we live. Doctrines with no traction in everyday life are just hot air and a tragic waste of time and paper and brain cells. As the Bible warns: "Faith by itself, if it is not accompanied by action, is dead" (James 2:17).

So how do the emphases of the Reformed version of the Christian faith make a difference in everyday living? We're glad you asked.

Here are six "E"s that distinguish Reformed practice:

- Embodied
- Elder led
- Ecumenical
- Education oriented
- Easter observing
- Equity seeking

Embodied

Many Christians consider themselves to be individual followers of Jesus who may or may not decide voluntarily to join other Christians in celebrating or living out the faith. They have a personalized faith that focuses somewhat exclu-

PAUSE

The Reformed tradition at its worst can concentrate so hard on obeying God's will that it becomes downright legalistic. So instead of giving others a heart full of God's encouraging good news in Jesus Christ, it has often given them an earful of stinging criticism instead. Not a pretty practice or one we should continue! At its best, though, the Reformed tradition practices the faithful exercise of mutual discipline. Disciples of Jesus disciple each other—on our journey through life we keep showing each other the way. We need to tell each other the truth, but must always do so in love.

SO WHAT

Can I be a Christian even though I don't attend church? I suppose. It's your faith in Jesus, not your church attendance, by which you are saved. But you're clearly violating your Savior's will for you if you don't take up your place in the body of Christ: "Let us not give up meeting together, as some are in the habit of doing, but let us encourage one another—and all the more as you see the Day approaching" (Hebrews 10:25).

sively on their own beliefs, needs, wants, and relationship to the Lord. Reformed believers find that sad. They confess that they have been adopted to be living members of God's family— of the church. They can't understand how believers could possibly want to keep themselves outside of the body of Christ.

Like any family, God's family on earth has its problems. It's not always easy to cooperate with our sisters and brothers in the Lord. We're all different. We have our own likes and dislikes, our own opinions, our own ways of doing things. But God's Word clearly points out that God's vision for us is to be a family that stays together, prays together, and even plays together. And in Matthew 28:18-20 our risen Lord has made it abundantly clear what our common mission is—to disciple not just ourselves, but all the nations of the world. To achieve that we cannot just crawl into our own little corner to let our light shine. We'll need to work *together,* empowered by God's Spirit and led by our risen Lord.

If only we would listen more carefully to the apostle Paul:

> As a prisoner for the Lord, then, I urge you to live a life worthy of the calling you have received. Be completely humble and gentle; be patient, bearing with one another in love. Make every effort to keep the unity of the Spirit through the bond of peace. There is one body and one Spirit— just as you were called to one hope when you were called—one Lord, one

faith, one baptism; one God and
Father of all, who is over all and
through all and in all.

—Ephesians 4:1-6

So how do we know Paul was talking here about
the church? In verse one he pounds it home.
Three times in a single sentence he uses the
Greek word for "call." Literally translated, Paul's
words say: "I *call* you to live a life worthy of the
calling with which you were *called.*" *Ekklesia*, the
Greek word for *church*, literally means "the
called-out ones." Believers are called out of the
bleeding, cancerous, hell-bound mess of humanity to become living members of Christ's glorious body on earth. As individual believers we are
embodied into a faith, and Spirit, and people,
and family that are much bigger than just individual little islands of faith. We're part of the
holy, worldwide church of Jesus Christ.

Our shared faith in Jesus, the Holy Spirit within
us, and our love for one another will make us
clump together as naturally and necessarily as
the cells of any body. Believers don't only *go* to
church. They *are* the church! For better or
worse, our Lord clearly *calls* us to be in this
together.

Elder Led
There are three main ways in which churches
organize themselves in this world: top down,
bottom up, and balanced between the two.

Churches like the Roman Catholic, Anglican
(Episcopalian), and Eastern Orthodox Churches
organize themselves from the top down. They

believe that Jesus gives full spiritual authority to one earthly representative to rule over the church. Let's use the Roman Catholic Church as an example. The person entrusted with full authority is called the pope. The pope needs other church leaders to help him govern the church, so he appoints cardinals, who, in turn, with the pope's consent, appoint bishops. Bishops, again with the consent of the pope and the cardinals, ordain priests, who have spiritual rule over the local church. Priests will enlist the services of fellow believers to conduct all the ministries of the local church.

Top-down churches function like an army. The soldiers of the cross are governed by successively smaller groups of leaders. They all receive their authority from those above them—and ultimately from the pope himself. And the pope receives his authority directly from Christ, the king of the church.

Bottom-up churches are structured more like a democracy. Local church pastors are chosen by the common consent of the local church membership and given authority to lead the church. But the membership retains the right to revoke this authority at any time. Congregations may decide to join associations of other churches and even join together to form a denomination. But these associations and denominations have no inherent authority of their own. So while top-down churches place the weight of authority on the side of denominational leaders, the bottom-up churches place it on the opposite side—that of the local church membership.

An Intermediate Model

Reformed/Presbyterian churches attempt to balance these two leadership styles by using a model of church government they find in the New Testament.

The Bible portrays the early church as being elder-led. Elders were appointed in every congregation and were put in charge on the local level. The apostle Paul explicitly instructs the evangelist Titus to appoint elders in every town. And Paul insists that the elders who direct the affairs of the church well are worthy of double honor (1 Timothy 5:17). And it's elders who ordain and empower pastors in their ministry by the laying on of hands (1 Timothy 4:14). So Reformed churches are not a pure democracy. They're more like a republic. In tune with the Spirit's leading, believers in these churches set apart for service those who will lead them according to God's Word. The congregation then entrusts leadership to the elders. The elders may certainly consult with the membership on important issues. But the final decisions are ultimately made in the council room.

In most Reformed churches pastors are considered to be preaching/teaching elders. They work along with the elders in providing spiritual leadership and pastoral care to the members of the congregation. Beyond that they have the specific task of proclaiming and teaching God's Word, serving the sacraments, and leading communal worship. Pastors are accountable to the elders for their work.

Most Reformed/Presbyterian churches also ordain deacons. Deacons usually serve along with the elders and pastors in the council or session. This assembly usually gives leadership to most of the life and work of the congregation. Deacons are specifically called to lead the congregation in showing Christ's loving care and concern for those in need both within and outside of the church.

The Bible also reveals that congregations often cooperated, assisted each other, and came together to make mutual decisions on items of common interest. Yet no congregation lorded it over any other (see 1 Peter 5:3). So while congregations have their own unique authority to govern themselves, they are also called to work together for the common good, recognizing that Jesus commands the church on earth to be one. So while original authority resides with the council/session of the local church, regional and denominational assemblies are delegated authority to deal with matters of shared ministry and mutual accountability.

Individual Christians are directly called and authorized by Christ to fulfill their calling. But that calling includes joining together in the fellowship of believers. So believers entrust authority over their mutual fellowship to elders, pastors, and deacons. In turn, individual congregations are called to join together with other congregations to work together as Christ's body. So local churches entrust regional and denominational assemblies with authority to give leadership in matters of common mission and concern as well.

Ecumenical

Reformed churches are ecumenical. That's the opposite of sectarian. A Christian sect asserts that it alone is the true church and that everybody else belongs to the false church. Reformed churches believe that they are only one small part of a much larger body of believers that together make up the one worldwide body of Christ on earth. So Reformed churches may look differently, think differently, and even act differently than other members of God's family, but those differences don't make them think that they're the only members of the family. In fact, they're convinced that their heavenly Father wants them to get along so well that they will work together to bring the good news of Jesus Christ far and wide.

Maybe we can't iron out all our differences with Roman Catholics or Pentecostals just yet. That shouldn't keep us from trying. We preach the same gospel of Jesus Christ and him crucified and risen. We share in the same Spirit and celebrate two of the same sacraments. We disciple each other to follow the same Savior and Lord. So we know that we're called to work together even if we can't always worship together. And we long, pray, and work for the wonderful day when we can do that too.

Education Oriented

Reformed churches are big on biblical teaching—sometimes to a fault. But that eagerness arises directly from their emphasis on the authority of the Bible and on God's claim on every part of our life. The Bible won't be able to guide us in our thinking or acting if we don't know what it says or what it means. And it's not

SO WHAT

A real strength of the Reformed/Presbyterian system of church government is how it keeps everybody accountable. No believer is an island. Elders visit church members to encourage them in their Christian walk and to help them find direction when they wander off the path. Councils/presbyteries hold pastors accountable. Church councils receive visits from representatives of wider assemblies to help them review their ministry. Reformed churches are now experimenting with new ways to hold one another accountable: small groups, coaching, mentoring, and so on. Reformed churches still need to be constantly reforming.

FACTOID

There are a lot more ways in which churches work together than you might think, including working together in interdenominational assemblies and agencies. If you've got a real burden on your heart for working toward the unity of Christ's body, talk to your pastor, elder, or deacon about where you might make a valuable contribution.

enough just to know the Bible; we also have to train ourselves to live the Bible. So the emphasis on teaching shows up in a lot of different ways in Reformed circles. Here are just a few:

- *Emphasis on preaching in worship.* The sermon is a central focus in Reformed worship services. Reformed churches insist on well-trained pastors who carefully explain and apply God's Word to the congregation every Sunday.

- *A second service.* Traditionally Reformed churches have adopted the Reformation practice of offering two worship services each Sunday. The second service is intended to specifically focus on teaching.

- *Church education.* Reformed churches offer a wide variety of classes and small-group studies specifically tuned to the needs and learning styles of young and old, seeker and mature Christian, farmer and professor. Discipleship is seen as a lifelong calling, not something that ends once we've made public profession of our faith.

- *Family worship.* When believers present their children for baptism they are asked to make a number of promises. One of those promises is that they will nurture their children in God's ways. Parents are held accountable for their role in raising their children up "in the fear of the Lord."

- *Christian day schools, colleges, and seminaries.* Because we confess that our world belongs to God, Reformed churches promote the development of schools and institutions that offer a solid Bible-based education. Christian schools are an important way in which believers are educated and equipped to take up their role in God's kingdom. Believers are called by their Lord to be imagebearers of God in their work, their worship, their family life, their social involvement, and their recreation. Learning to be citizens of God's kingdom is a full-time calling. Christian schools provide an excellent way for students to heed that calling in all its many dimensions.

Easter Observing

Reformed Christians gather together for worship on Sunday because the Bible teaches that on Sunday Jesus Christ rose from the dead (Matthew 24:1). The Bible also teaches that in response to that event believers shifted their focus from Saturday/Sabbath worship to Sunday worship (Acts 20:7).

God commanded his people to rest on the seventh day, the end of the week, to celebrate the completion of the work of creation. But because of our sin, the creation was plunged into ruin. But Jesus, the firstfruits of the new creation, arose on the first day of the week to begin the eternal sabbath. As he demonstrated in his sabbath healings, with his arrival as Lord of the sabbath, every day of the week is now a sabbath day! Every day is now a day hallowed and devoted to the service of God. So while every day is suitable for worship, Reformed churches still favor Sunday, because it lets them follow New Testament custom and celebrate Easter over and over again, every week.

WORD ALERT

God's kingdom is God's active rule in the world. Before we fell into sin, God's rule was everywhere. After we sinned, Satan enslaved much of God's good creation, including our own sin-imprisoned hearts. In Christ God has again begun to reestablish his active reign over us as persons, over our families and communities, and over this fallen creation. We long for the great day when King Jesus will return, free us all from the tyranny of the devil, and fully establish his glorious and gentle reign over all creation once more.

So whenever they do worship together, what's "Reformed" about Reformed worship? Here are a few distinctives:

- The purpose of worship is twofold: to bring to God the glory our Lord deserves and to build ourselves up in the faith.

- The Word of God read and faithfully proclaimed is one central focus of the service. The celebration of the sacraments is the second. We require our ministers to be well-educated, diligent, and obedient to Scripture in applying the Word to our lives. Elders are responsible for supervising our communal worship, but all members are responsible for participating in worship, praying for those who preach and lead, and sharing the Word with others.

- The participation of the congregation is very important—in worship God speaks, and we respond in faith. Nothing is allowed to intrude into the service that interferes with this genuine conversation of God with the rest of the family.

- Reformed worship is trinitarian, addressing Father, Son, and Holy Spirit—and celebrating the many and various works of God in creation, redemption, and sanctification.

- While worship styles differ, we affirm the importance of a balanced diet of singing psalms, hymns shared by believers across the world/centuries, and new songs that allow us to celebrate the freshness of God's deeds.

- We tend to gather twice on Sundays to worship God.

Equity Seeking

Contemporary North American Christianity tends to be divided into two camps: the "evangelicals" and the "mainliners." Evangelicals stress the importance of having a personal, saving relationship with Jesus Christ while mainliners stress the biblical call to do justice. Evangelicals concentrate on evangelizing people and saving their souls. Mainliners concentrate on saving people from poverty and oppression.

So how about Reformed Christians? Are they evangelicals or mainliners? The short answer is that they are both. With the evangelicals they emphasize the importance of developing a personal, saving relationship with Jesus Christ. Without that our faith is only a worthless shell. But with the mainliners, Reformed Christians equally stress the global ramifications of that personal relationship with Jesus: it calls us to a life of discipleship in which we claim all of life for God's kingdom. Jesus is good news for the heart of every sinner. Jesus is also good news for the whole world.

So Reformed Christians involve themselves in personal evangelism with the same zeal as they engage in social action. Reformed churches do outreach to win unbelievers to Christ. They send out missionaries to every corner of the globe to proclaim Jesus Christ to all who will believe. But they also work hard at providing for the needs of the homeless and the hungry. They call and work for justice and equity in their neighborhoods and around the world. They work hard at

FACTOID

Reformed Christians tackle the task of working for social justice in different ways. One way is to work within the structures of society—say, within one or another existing political party. Another way is to create a distinctly Christian presence, such as a Christian labor union, a Christian political party, or an interdenominational Christian task force. The same issue arises as to whether it's best to provide Christian education for children within the context of the public schools or whether we should send them to Christian schools. While we may certainly maintain and advocate for our own convictions on this, I'm glad to see that there is a growing consensus to support the notion that we can applaud them both. These are not mutually exclusive. God's Word can find many avenues into our lives and into our society. Let's not be too eager to tell the Spirit what to do and how to do it. Better for us to concentrate on staying in step with the Spirit (Galatians 5:25).

opposing racism and seek to liberate those who are oppressed. They serve others with Word and deed. They are the mouth of Christ and the hands of Christ. We realize that we *can* talk and work at the same time. Jesus showed us how.

A Parting Thought

We've only scratched the surface in this brief survey of the Reformed faith. Undoubtedly I've left a lot of material out. I've oversimplified and maybe even misrepresented. But that's inevitable when we try to reduce into print the riches and variability of a living, breathing, growing, dynamic tradition. I do hope and pray you've found it a worthwhile exercise nevertheless, and I encourage you to keep on learning more. I firmly believe that your ongoing study and practice of Reformed teachings will do what they are intended to do—to plant your nose more often in the living pages of Scripture and your spiritual feet ever more securely and productively on our solid Rock. May you grow in grace! To God be the glory.

Because it's so easy to leave material out or to oversimplify, I thought, to be on the safe side, I would include snippets of an excellent alternate presentation of what it means to be Reformed. My pastor, Rev. Duane Kelderman, preached a series of sermons at Neland Avenue Christian Reformed Church in which he presented sixteen words or phrases that summarize Reformed teaching. You'll find them in Appendix C.

Points to Ponder

1. Does belonging to the church mean more than that we attend worship services? If so, what does it mean?

2. Does the church have authority over us? If so, what kind?

3. Whose responsibility is Christian education? How should that responsibility be fulfilled?

4. What is worship? How do we know if we're doing it right?

5. If we refuse to help the poor and needy in Christ's name, can we still go to heaven?

6. What struck me the most about Reformed teaching is . . .

7. What questions do you still have about being Reformed? Where do you want to go from here?

Our Church Neighborhood

On page 66 is an overview of the tree that constitutes the major divisions of Christ's church on earth. The tree is rooted in Christ and in Christ's Word. But it has split up into a bewildering amount of branches and sub-branches. This chart provides only a bird's-eye view. The reality is much more complicated. Continue to pray for the unity and the faithfulness of the church.

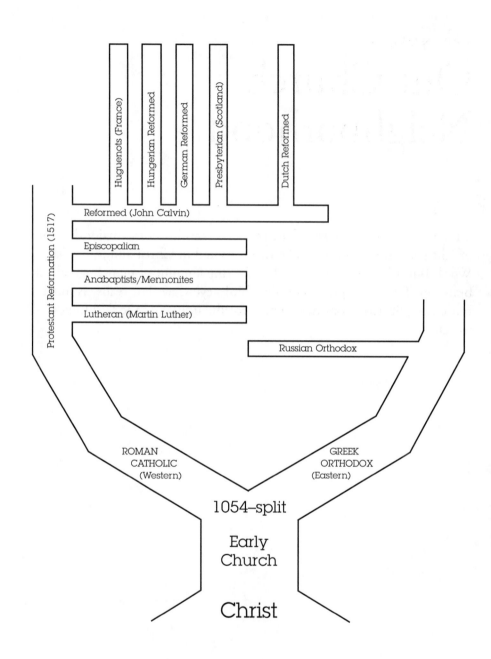

Huguenots (France)
Hungarian Reformed
German Reformed
Presbyterian (Scotland)
Dutch Reformed

Reformed (John Calvin)

Protestant Reformation (1517)

Episcopalian

Anabaptists/Mennonites

Lutheran (Martin Luther)

Russian Orthodox

ROMAN
CATHOLIC
(Western)

GREEK
ORTHODOX
(Eastern)

1054–split

Early
Church

Christ

—Cornelius Plantinga, *A Sure Thing*, teacher's manual (Grand Rapids: CRC Publications, 2001), p. 146

Creeds, Confessions, and Doctrinal Standards

Reformed churches and Presbyterian churches share three creeds with most other Christian churches. These are

- The Apostolic (Apostles') Creed
- The Nicene Creed
- The Athanasian Creed

While not all churches have formally adopted any or all of these, they do accurately summarize the central beliefs that are held by all Christ-confessing churches.

Many Reformed churches have adopted three doctrinal standards that summarize more specifically the teachings that characterize these churches:

- The Belgic Confession
- The Heidelberg Catechism
- The Canons of Dort

While Presbyterian churches agree with the teachings of these doctrinal standards, they have not formally adopted them. For historical reasons they have their own set of confessions. Those confessions that are accepted by most Presbyterian churches (with minor subsequent amendments) are those that were adopted by the assembly of divines meeting at Westminster from 1643-47:

- The Confession of Faith
- The Larger Catechism
- The Shorter Catechism

A number of Presbyterian denominations have adopted subsequent statements instead of or in addition to these. For example, the PCUSA has adopted "The Brief Statement of Faith" and a new set of catechisms.

In responding to the unique challenges of faith presented by the times in which we live, a number of Reformed and Presbyterian churches have formulated statements of faith that directly address idols of our age such as secularism, individualism, and relativism. For example, the Reformed Church in America offers a contemporary statement of faith called "Our Song of Hope." The Christian Reformed Church has adopted a similar statement called "Our World Belongs to God: A Contemporary Testimony."

To find out more about the beliefs of Reformed and Presbyterian churches, visit their web sites. With a bit of on-screen navigating, you will find a listing of their core beliefs. Here are just a few web sites to get you started. This is by no means a complete or even an inclusive listing.

- The Christian Reformed Church: www.crcna.org
- The Reformed Church in America: www.rca.org
- The Presbyterian Church (U.S.A): www.pcusa.org
- The Evangelical Presbyterian Church: www.epc.org
- The Orthodox Presbyterian Church: www.opc.org
- The Presbyterian Church in Canada: www.presbyterian.ca

Happy hunting!

Sixteen Keywords

Here are sixteen words or phrases that Rev. Duane Kelderman uses to characterize Reformed teaching. He groups them under three categories, which indicate three separate streams of thought within the Reformed tradition. These streams of thought are not antithetical to each other, but they represent different emphases that, taken together, allow for a robust and balanced Reformed expression of the Christian faith.

Kelderman's three categories are

- *The Doctrinalist Emphasis*—a strong adherence to certain Christian doctrines as taught in the Scriptures and reflected in the confessions of the church.

- *The Pietist Emphasis*—careful attention to the Christian life and to one's personal relationship to God.

- *The Transformationalist Emphasis*—a heartfelt desire to relate the lordship of Christ to all areas of culture, to society, and to the world around us.

Here are the sixteen words or phrases Kelderman suggests that fit under these three headings. Regrettably, to save space, I've had to severely truncate his excellent discussion of these words.

Doctrinalist Emphases

1. *Scripture* (2 Timothy 3:16)—the Reformed faith has a high view of Scripture: the Bible is the inspired, infallible, authoritative Word of God.

2. *Grace* (Ephesians 2:8-10)—the Reformed faith gives us a deep understanding of how radical and pervasive our sinful condition is and how radically and totally our salvation is a gift of God.

3. *Creation-Fall-Redemption-Recreation* (Colossians 1:15-20)—this is the way Reformed Christians understand the biblical message in the light of redemptive history.

4. *Covenant* (Jeremiah 31:31-34)—Reformed Christians see the Old Testament and the New Testament as revealing God's relationship to us as one covenant of grace spanning from God's promise to Adam and Eve to the new city of God described in Revelation 22.

5. *Common Grace* (Matthew 5:43-48)—in distinction from saving grace, common grace refers to that attitude of divine favor that extends to humanity in general, believers and unbelievers alike.

Pietist Emphases

6. *Personal Relationship to Jesus* (Romans 8:38-39)—the heart of our faith is our personal relationship to Jesus Christ, which alone can give us peace, hope, and courage.

7. *The Holy Spirit* (Romans 8:1-17)—a renewed appreciation for the person and work of the Holy Spirit—the giver of spiritual life and the one who empowers our ministry.

8. *Gratitude* (Colossians 3:15-17)—Reformed Christians identify this as our key motivator for living the Christian life according to God's will.

9. *The Church* (Ephesians 4:1-16)—Reformed Christians hold strongly that to belong to Christ *is* to belong to those who belong to Christ.

10. *Word and Deed* (James 2:14-17)—when we talk about the mission of the church, we're talking about Word and deed: proclaiming the gospel and ministering to those in need.

Transformationalist Emphases

11. *Jesus Is Lord* (Philippians 2:11)—Reformed Christians counter the secular worldview in confessing the Lordship of Jesus over all of life.

12. *Kingdom* (Matthew 6:10)—the kingdom of God is the rule of God over all things, vindicated and reestablished once and for all in the death and resurrection of Jesus Christ.

13. *The Cultural Mandate* (Genesis 1:27-28)—as imagebearers of God, we humans exercise dominion over God's world and are called to do so in a stewardly, God-honoring way.

14. *Christian Education* (Proverbs 9:10)—we believe that Christ is Lord of all of life, including all spheres of learning. True education includes God as the Creator and Lord of all things and integrates Christ into all facets of learning.

15. *Christian Vocation* (Ephesians 4:28)—Reformed Christians view their entire life, not just Sunday and church life, as a divine calling. This includes their time, their daily work, their giftedness, their wealth, and their recreation.

16. *Justice* (Micah 6:8)—Reformed Christians pursue biblical justice, which is characterized as righteousness, uprightness, the restoring of relationships, the righting of wrongs, all of which lead to shalom and obedience to God's law.

A Three-Point Summary

Kelderman concludes by offering three brief statements that further summarize these sixteen phrases. Once again, remember that they form a package deal:

1. To be Reformed is to appreciate the radical depth of our sin and of God's grace.

2. To be Reformed is to know that our only comfort is that we belong to Jesus.

3. To be Reformed is to appreciate the radical breadth of Christ's lordship and to submit our whole self to his rule.